Copyright ⓒ James Ejeh, 2016

ISBN - 978-978-54171-1-1

Published by

REFORMATION BOOKS

Reformation House,

Otukpo, Benue State, Nigeria

E-mail: reformationhouse2013@gmail.com

Telephone: 08168379238, 08183980039

All scripture quotations are taken from the AUTHORISED KING JAMES VERSION unless otherwise indicated.

Table of Contents

Dedication

This book is dedicated to all Christians who sincerely are longing to see and experience the real power of God and manifest same to silence all the false manifestations that we have around today.

APPRECIATION

First, I want to thank and appreciate the Almighty God for helping me to see and experience the grace of God that brought me salvation and for making me a partaker of the inheritance of the saints in light and secondly for counting me faithful putting me in the ministry of the gospel and for giving me a voice through writing.

I also want to appreciate several men and women whose lives and ministries have affected me at one point or the other, among whom are the two men that God used to teach me the fundamentals of the faith, namely Evang. Emmanuel Ibrahim and Pastor Ameh Amana. Particularly, I want to thank God's servant Evang, Emmanuel Ibrahim, who in spite his busy schedules accepted to write the forward of this book. Sir, the Lord bless you for sparing your time.

I will not forget also the ministry of Uncle Gbile Akanni which I was privileged to come in contact with early in my Christian faith. I actually don't know him closely but his several conferences and teaching materials have really helped me to maintain biblical Christianity which I am an advocate. Mrs. Rebecca Audu popularly known as Mummy Rebecca was a great encouragement to me during my growing years in the faith. God bless you for your motherly watch.

Drs Steve Ogah and Kotein Trinya are both powerful Christian writers who through their Christian writers' seminar in Portharcourt taught me the elementary of publishing which has greatly enhanced my writing ministry; I want to appreciate them for their contribution to this aspect of my ministry. I appreciate the ministries of two men which I got in touch with recently. They are the teaching ministry of Pastor Dotun of the kingdom Citizen Pavilion, Jos and that of Apostle Arome Osayi of the Christian Remnant Network, Makurdi.

Both ministries came when I was struggling with certain persuasion of mine. Gideon Odoma of the Fortress ministry, Jos is another young man whose school of Apologetics has revolutionized my thinking, I appreciate you, sir!

My appreciation also goes to several brethren who have been part of my ministry at one point or the other and especially to Bro. Sunday Idoko, his wife, Kate and Bro. Simon Abih who have endured with me in my struggle as a minister. When others left, they stood by me; a hundred fold of blessings await them now and eternity. Worthy of note also is the contributions of Dr Moses Daniel of St. Daniel Hospital. I have met only a few of his caliber who understand the kingdom life like him.

I appreciate my three daughters, Confidence, Marvelous and Peniel who in spite of my several inabilities have loved and appreciated me as their father. Their resilient spirit is highly commendable. I love you girls! Finally, Many thanks to my dear wife who always have to travel hundreds of miles from her station just to show me that she cares even when it is most inconvenient for her. Thanks for your loveliness. Blessed are you among women!

FORWARD

Everything around us is clear witness to the fact that there is a powerful God behind the entirety of creation. Our Father is not a weak, impotent, empty and powerless God. He is the source, centre and author of power (Ps. 62:11). If power belongs to God, then it is very absurd that His church is so feeble in our time. The church that started in power cannot survive without it.

The power bankruptcy massively evident in the body of Christ today is not only retarding the advancement of our kingdom but making a mockery of the cross. A lot of the victims of hell are forced to look elsewhere for help since the accredited channels of hope are unable to deliver Calvary dividends to ailing humanity.

If satanic counterfeits must not overshadow the original works of the Holy Ghost, bearers of genuine fire must arise now. God is willing and able to restore apostolic mantle back to the church, if men who angry at their emptiness will rise to pay the price for unction. Being angry at emptiness and hungry for fullness are the two catalysts of virtue release.

God's servant James Ejeh is a man sold out to God and passionate about the restoration of the church to her position of purity, purpose and power. God has used him to meticulously and elaborately discuss this critical and timely matter, in this spirit motivated and monitored book.

He did not write as one exempted from this dearth but in a graphic manner showed us how he personally travailed and of course still travails, to lay hold on the full grace of God. This is a book that if read well will surely keep you on your knees until you are engulfed in fire from above. It will help you to groan for grace.

This is one book that will not show your need alone but dwelt greatly on what you can do to attain and retain the supernatural. I encourage all Christian leaders in particular and Christians in general to read this book. However, for maximum impact, it must be read prayerfully.

Understanding the supernatural is a valuable resource material for churches, Bible Colleges and those committed to disciple making.

It is our prayer that this book will make you restless until you are soaked in the spirit. May it positively adjust your speed in your pursuit of God. May it make you hate powerlessness to the point that you are ready to get the mantle at whatever cost.

I wish you an unforgettable encounter with the spirit and the Word, as you read this book.

Evang. Emmanuel Ibrahim

Outreach African Mission,

Anyigba, Nigeria.

PREFACE

Sometimes ago, I was discussing with a brother rcently and one dominant issue on our discussion was the absence of the supernatural from the midst of God's people. I was like saying, what will be my fate when I stand before the judgment seat of Christ only with a blood-washed life, but with nothing to show for what the blood has purchased me? You know it's a terrible condition to find yourself. Paul said in Philippians 3:12 that he was apprehended by Christ to also apprehend something. I came to understand that I was not just redeemed for nothing but for something. I was redeemed to demonstrate the glory of God. I mean we are all saved to demonstrate the saving power of Christ, in other words we are saved to serve for the salvation of humanity under the influence of the supernatural.

Somebody said, "you are not truly saved if your salvation is not saving others. You are not truly blessed if your blessing is not blessing others". To me, this is something to seriously think upon, because I believe that everyone who has truly been saved is entitled to all that Calvary stands for, including the supernatural manifestation of the power of God.

All over the world, there is this general quest for more, more of everything that is attainable. The politicians crave for higher positions. The businessmen are searching for more strategies of success in their businesses, the youth for more knowledge, criminal for more strategies of operation. Religious sects all over the world are craving for recognition. I have heard of a Muslim fanatic in South Africa who claimed to have undergone a twenty-one-day fast. What was he looking for? I suppose he was looking for more power to manifest evils to counterfeit the power of God.

My point is that the whole world is getting dissatisfied with where they are in every sphere of life (politically, socially, mentally, economically and spiritually) and everybody is crying for more. And let me be honest with you, the way the world is advancing in power, if you don't have something superior, something from God, you are not likely to survive as a Christian in the coming days. As Christians and especially as ministers of the gospel and as ambassadors of Christ here on earth (1Corrinthians 5:20), what should be our own heart cry and craving at this point in time? And to you particularly, what is it that is consuming you up? These and other questions are tackled in this book. I am believing and trusting God that a hunger for the authentic supernatural will burst forth upon your spirit before you finish going through this 'HUNGER MOTIVATOR' in Jesus' name. Amen. God bless you and happy reading.

James Ejeh

CHAPTER ONE

THE POWER FROM ON HIGH

Each time, I hear stories of false prophets who claim to have the power of God and how people troop to them for solutions; I realize why we (the church) need the supernatural to hold the world together. These false prophets with these magical powers under the influence of familiar spirits and sorceries all over the places attract customers from both within and outside the church. Why are these magicians getting this much attention? Why are they holding sway this way? I believe that it is because, though they are false, they have something though counterfeit which the church lacks.

Any time I remember the absence of the power of God in the church, I cry to God that He in His infinite mercy will visit us again. I am trying to look at the needs that abound in our world today so that we can all appreciate the level of the supernatural that is needed in the church today. Because, it is the prevailing needs that call for supernatural manifestation. You just need to read the dailies, tune to several so called Christian Television channels and travel to cities and villages around the world and you will understand my vintage point.

Prayer and prophecy houses are littered all over the places operated by sorcerers and people with familiar spirits, people who have no connection with God, because the church that was commissioned with the mandate to go and "heal the sick, cleanse the lepers, raise the dead, cast out the devils"(Matttew.10:8) has greatly fallen short of this heaven-given mandate and privilege as a result of which great credence has been given to all the false manifestations of the devil's powers that we have around.

But instead of us to acknowledge our emptiness and our inadequacies, I see many of us so satisfied with empty tongue speaking that cannot even intimidate flies.

THE REASON FOR THE POWER

Let's try and look at the reason why Jesus warned the disciples not to try to preach the gospel but to wait in Jerusalem until they have been endued with the power from on high. Below were His last words to His chosen apostles before He was received up to heaven;

"But ye shall receive power after that the Holy Ghost is come upon you; and ye shall be witnesses unto me both in Jerusalem, and in all Judea, and in Samaria, and unto the uttermost part of the earth" Acts 1:8

Jesus saw the need to leave behind an empowered church that will take care of the several needs in Jerusalem, Judea, Samaria and all the rest of the world. He realized that nothing short of a "power from on high" (Lk.24:49) would be needed by these ordinary fishermen and tax collector turned-apostles to effectively minister to their sin, sickness and judgment-bound generation. Jesus knew that Jerusalem was a place where no one goes and leaves scot-free without a taste of persecution. He realized that nothing short of a power from on high could stand the heat of Jerusalem's persecution.

If not for the power of God on Jesus, how could He have endured the cruel death on Calvary's cross? If not for the power of God which Paul encountered on his way to Damascus, (Acts 9:1-6) and several other subsequent encounters which he had, how could he have stood the terrible persecution which came upon him at Jerusalem and all the Gentile cities where he went to minister (See Acts 21). If not the power of God from on high, who could have preached in Samaria a city noted for idolatry and adultery and have any effective ministry such as Philip demonstrated? What could have brought "a great joy" (Acts 8:8) to the city of Samaria and what could have set the people free from the hold of false spirits under the leadership of men like Simon the sorcerer if not the power of God manifested through His yielded vessel Philip, an ordinary Deacon(Acts 8:5-13).

The point am trying to make here is that Jesus knew the peculiar needs of the various places He mentioned in Acts 1:8, (namely Jerusalem, all Judea, Samarian and the uttermost part of the earth) and the level of power that could change the conditions of these places, hence His charge to the disciples to stay in the city until you have been clothed with power from on high Luke 24:49(NIV).

THE UPPER CHAMBER

Now, did the disciples ignore this final instruction? They didn't, why? Because this instruction is from the Man to Whom belong all power (Psalm 62:11). Rather, in obedience, they went in sincerity and in hunger to the designated place, the upper room where they shut themselves in for the promised power from on high.

I have to make an observation here: though there were many other rooms in Jerusalem; the instruction was specifically to go to 'the upper room' (Acts 1:13). Though there was the temple in Jerusalem, the normal place of prayer, Jesus did not recommend it to the disciples but 'the upper room'. So the disciples in obedience forsook every other room in Jerusalem and went into the upper room. This is giving me a serious understanding; and that is the power we need cannot be gotten from anywhere but the upper room. I believe the upper room symbolizes heaven or the presence of God.

Many are going around seeking for power from sorcerers to get attention in their ministries, many go to rivers to acquire powers, and many even go to sleep among the tombs to receive power. But as far as I am concerned, the kind of power that will minister to the total man (soul, spirit and body) can never come from any other source except from the upper room (the very presence of God). No power less than the power from on high can make any lasting impact on the lives of men.

There are other genuine believers whose faith rest only in the laying on of hands of other anointed men and women of God. Others believe that they have to sow a seed into the life of a particular man of God they desire his anointing and they will automatically come into it. I believe in impartation. I also believe in sowing seed into the lives of genuine men of God. But I believe that the kind of power we need to affect our generation must come through personal encounter with the Almighty God who is the only one who gives power. As much as we need impartation from senior ministers, I think also that personal encounter in the "upper room" is most vital to our manifesting the glory of Jehovah.

When the five foolish virgins demanded for oil from the wise ones in the parable of the ten virgins, what was their response?

But the wise answered, saying, Not so; lest there be not enough for us and you: but go rather to them that sell, and buy for yourselves (Matthew. 25:9).

The five wise virgins told the five foolish ones to go to the source of the oil and buy for themselves because when it comes to the issue of oil which actually represents grace, it is a personal matter. Everyone must go to God for acquisition.

BLESSED ARE THE HUNGRY

Who are those that are entitled to this power from on high? Though I know that the power of God is available for every professor of the Christian faith, but I believe also that there is a price to pay for us to have access to the real power of the living Christ. In the gospel according to St. Matthew chapter five and in the sixth verse, the bible declares that:

Blessed are those who hunger and thirst for righteousness, for they will be filled (NIV).

The above scripture is clear. Anything from God is only received by men who value it and who really want it and this is manifested in their hunger and thirst. Whether it is righteousness, or power or anything that you want from God, it is exclusively reserved for those who hunger and thirst for it. I hear the Spirit of the Lord saying to the church that 'blessed are they that do hunger'. That is like saying that the only people that can be blessed with this upper room power are those with genuine hunger for God. Naturally speaking it's only a hungry child who cries for food that gets the attention of his mother. It is not different in spiritual matters.

All who were genuinely used of God in the past were all men of intense hunger for God. Genuine hunger is the only passage I know into the power of God. But this is an attribute greatly lacking in our lives today. Many like the biblical Eutychus have fallen into deep sleep and are already waiting for their spiritual death. Many of us are sitting on windows with no defined stand in the faith. We are not inside, neither are we outside, one leg inside and one leg outside. Many Christians are rather too satisfied and comfortable with ordinary church ceremonies and activities that could only at best earn them the name of good Christians. But let me tell you, the truth is that an empty good Christian cannot change his world, but a powerful Christian can, that is the difference!

Christians of today are so cold, no zeal for God or the things of God. We have no Christians who will cry to God to send us His power as of old, the kind that can turn the heart of men to God. All we have are people with hunger for the pleasures of life. But I believe that before you finish reading through these pages, you will catch the supernatural power of God in Jesus' name.

A HUNGRY MAN IS AN ANGRY MAN

Of late I became too dissatisfied, critical and even angry with everything that happens in the church today. Sometimes I have had to check my spirit if am becoming too extreme in my observation and reaction. But the Holy Spirit keeps assuring me that some of these observations and reactions are right and necessary. So, I discover that my case is that of a hungry man that is always angry.

Beloved, you can't have a genuine hunger for God and not be angry with the emptiness in the Body of Christ presently. In fact, when I began to receive the leading to resign from my secular assignment and make myself fully available for God's use, my fear had always been how to resign to face the same emptiness which many are not aware of, or have ignored. My cry day and night to God even before my resignation has been, "Lord, I am not just interested in being in ministry just for people to know I am in ministry but to experience your glory and to change my world with such a glory". And the answer of the Lord to me then always, was,

If you need the power that will make you a different man, then you need to know what others don't know and also do what others have failed or refused to do.

I tried to find out from the Lord what are those things that I need to know and do if I must manifest the supernatural power of God. The answer that came clearly to me then is what you are going to find out in the next chapter.

CHAPTER TWO

DIE TO LIVE

I have come across too many Christians who want to live in the flesh and operate in the supernatural. This is quite impossible. You can't eat your cake and have it. For,

"That which is born of the flesh is flesh and that which is born of the Spirit is spirit John". 3:6 (KJV)

The power of God is in the supernatural (spirit realm). The man of the flesh has no access into the supernatural. It is only the man of the spirit that can touch the supernatural. The man of the spirit is the one who lives in heaven on earth. So if a man must get hold of the power that will enable him operate beyond the natural, he must be ready to die to the natural and live in the supernatural. How do you know a man that lives in the supernatural? He evidently walks in the supernatural (Galatians 5:25).

There is a lot of manifestation of the flesh in what many of us call the power of God today. Too many of the manifestations we see around are often either contrary to scripture or mechanically manipulated. These have brought a lot of ridicules on our public ministries.

I know of several brethren who through such manipulation have earned themselves the title of Holy Ghost experts and deliverance specialists. When it comes to the challenge of Holy Ghost ministry and deliverance, these brethren are readily available. But a close look at their ministries show there is no genuine and lasting result of these ministries. Because, every genuine manifestation yields a lasting result with a living proof.

The flesh and the Spirit cannot walk together. They are always at enmity to each other.

"For the flesh desires what is contrary to the Spirit, and the Spirit what is contrary to the flesh. They are in conflict with each other" Galatians 5:17 (NIV).

And moreover, nothing genuine can result from the manifestation of the flesh because nothing good dwells in the realm of the flesh (Rom. 7:18). The option left for us then is either to die to the flesh and live the life of the supernatural or live for the flesh and forget the supernatural. That is the simple logic! The choice then is yours.

ARE YOU DEAD?

Any time I find myself praying and crying for the power of God, the question that always hits me from above is, "are you dead?" Any time I hear a Christian crying, "Lord, use me", the question that burns in my heart silently for such a Christian is always, "are you dead?" And I want to ask you this same question: are you dead or are you still alive to the flesh and want God to fill you with His power?

A DEAD MAN IS NOT CONSCIOUS OF THE NATURAL

Naturally speaking, what happens to you when you suddenly meet a man who you are quite aware had died and long buried walking towards you? You tremble and try to escape for your life. Why? Because it's abnormal for a dead man to walk and because you realize that a walking dead man must be operating beyond the natural world. It is the same with a believer who is dead to the flesh and the world. If you walk in this realm, your life becomes a threat to the devil and his people. All who encounter you must tremble because of your abnormality. I want to say here, that believers operating in this realm are always being looked upon as abnormal people or a different species of human beings. This is one parameter of knowing whether you are actually walking in the supernatural. If your life is such that everybody is still comfortable with your dealings, comfortable with your lifestyle, no questions about you and everybody is just in agreement with you, that is an attestation to the fact that you are still dwelling in the natural. Many times in the scripture you hear such questions as; "What manner of man is this?" or "Who is this?" or "What wisdom is this which is given to Him?" being asked about Jesus. This is because He lived an extra-ordinary life and did extra-ordinary deeds, so the natural men of His days could not quite comprehend the realm from whence he was operating. The truth is that the natural man is not supposed to understand the man of the Spirit according to the word of God.

The person without the Spirit does not accept the things that come from the Spirit of God but considers them foolishness, and cannot understand them because they are discerned only through the Spirit. 1Corrinthians 2:14 (NIV)

Like I said earlier on, when you see a dead man walking, he is being controlled by a supernatural force that enables him do anything physically impossible, yet not aware of what he is doing. This is because he is no longer alive to the natural world but alive in the supernatural. Sometimes when we walk in the realm of the supernatural, our lives can so much affect our natural environment without our knowing it, because we are no longer alive to the natural, but controlled by the supernatural to influence the natural. This is a mystery, but with our hearts opened to the Spirit of God, we can comprehend these things.

THE VOODOO MAGIC

I have heard of a town where corpses are controlled and used to labor on farm lands. This act is carried out by an occultic group known as 'voodoo'. These corpses (dead men) I learnt can do work that is beyond the scope of a living human being. This occultic group has contrived this demonic device to achieve their selfish ends because they have realized that a dead man is lifeless and therefore cannot complain, no matter the labor that he is engaged to do. When we walk as dead men, we can achieve a lot that naturally cannot be achieved.

God can only use dead men (dead to the flesh and the world) to demonstrate His life (the power of God) to this dying world. Men who are dead to the world and men of whom the world is no longer worthy (Galatians 6:14, Hebrew. 11:38), i.e. men who have said no to the world and its desires. These are men who will declare with the apostle Paul that:

I have been crucified with Christ and I no longer live, but Christ lives in me. The life I now live in the body, I live by faith in the Son of God, who loved me and gave Himself for me. Gal. 2:20 (NIV).

A HEAVENLY INJUNCTION

I want to ask you one question, have you come across any seed that germinates, grows and bear fruits without dying in the soil? I personally have not seen or heard of any seed that does not die in the ground before germinating. Though I have not studied much of science to see if such seed exists. But there is an injunction from the lips of the One by whom all things were created, the Omniscient, JESUS, the Son of the living God and what is that injunction?

"Very truly I tell you, unless a kernel of wheat falls to the ground and dies, it remains only a single seed. But if it dies, it produces many seeds" John 12:24 (NIV).

Friends, I want to charge you that except you want to live without the demonstration of God's power in your generation, otherwise, you must be ready to die. Let's quit trying to manage in the flesh and cry to God to give us the reality of His power. I have tried to study the Bible and several Christian histories to see if there was any one who lived and fulfilled God's purpose through the demonstration of His power who had not given up the flesh and I have found none. Here are a few examples:

THE LORD JESUS

The Lord Jesus Christ was a perfect example of a man that really demonstrated the power of God to His generation. He was a man who lived and changed the course of history through the demonstration of the power of the Most High God. He lived on this earth only for thirty-three years and six months and the world has never and can never recover from His brief appearance. Why and how was He granted access into such a realm that even satan recognized Him as the Son of God each time he encountered Him (Mark 5:6-7) The reason is simple; Jesus lived all His life fulfilling the will of His Father denying Himself of all His personal right and privileges. In several verses of the scriptures He alluded to that fact. For example in John 5:30 He said,

I can of mine own self do nothing: as I hear, I judge: and my judgment is just; because I seek not mine own will, but the will of the Father which hath sent me(KJV), and in John 6:38, He said,

"For I came down from heaven, not do mine own will, but the will of Him that sent me"(KJV).

So Jesus was able to subdue the world in such a very short time with the power of God, because He was completely dead to the world and its desires and fully alive to the will of His Father Who He represented. You can imagine that Satan took Him to the mountain and offered Him all the kingdom of the world and its glory, but He out rightly turned it down just to fulfill the will of His Father.

I hear my Savior say no to food even when He was obviously hungry and needed something to eat (Read Luke 4:1-13). Yet many of God's people have sold out their right to the power of God, for a few spoons of this world's pottage. No wonder, we are so short of the power of God today!

THE APOSTLE PAUL

This truth was also epitomized in the life of Paul one of the greatest apostles of Jesus Christ that ever lived. Paul was a man who sowed himself in the Spirit to die to the flesh and the world to become an embodiment of Christ's resurrection power. That power manifested so much through him that handkerchiefs from his body were casting devils and healing all manner of sicknesses and diseases. How did he come about such demonstration that enabled him turned his world upside down along side Silas, his companion in labor (Acts 17:6)? Philippians 3:7-10 gives the secret of this man's power.

 The seventh verse says:

"But whatever were gains to me I now consider loss for the sake of Christ" (NIV).

How many of us are ready to count everything loss that is gain to us? How many of us are ready to let go our affections for the sake of the power of God that we so desire. It was said that Paul was a doctor of law, highly esteemed by men of his time, was a man full of the righteousness of the law. But all these qualifications he considered:

"..a loss because of the surpassing worth of knowing Christ Jesus my Lord. Phil. 3:8 (NIV)

To Paul, the Excellency of the knowledge of Christ is greater than 'all things'.

How many of you know that the man with the power of God is a man of great excellence. As a matter of fact, those who are being addressed today in our society as Excellencies are actually not entitled to that title. The people qualified for such titles are Jesus Christ Himself, the Chief Excellency and His choice servants. On the contrary, what we are seeing is servants riding on horses while sons are walking on bare foot without heavenly boots to trample upon scorpions, snakes and the power of the devil as we have been mandated to do (Ecclesiastes 10:7 & Luke 10:19). It's unfortunate that God's servants today have become objects of ridicules and laughing stocks, because we are void of the supernatural power of God. May the Lord reverse that trend in the name of Jesus Christ.

So why did Paul take the risk of making the sacrifices of all his hard-earned rights? Philippians 3:10 says:

I want to know Christ - yes, to know the power of His resurrection and participation in His sufferings becoming like Him in His death (NIV).

Yes, until we know Christ this way that is to know Him in the power of His resurrection, to know Him in participation in His sufferings and to know Him in becoming like Him in His death, we have no access to the power and until we are ready to drop our personalities and live for Him alone, we can't know Him to that degree that will qualify us for the power. For the knowledge of God that introduces men to His power is only available to them who live for His will alone (John 7:17). The ancient song writer said:

But we never can prove

The delights of His love

Until all on the altar we lay;

For the favour He shows,

And the joy He bestows,

Are for them who will

trust and obey

Until we are ready to lay all (our rights and privileges, our titles, our pride, our names and our personalities) on the altar, we can never 'prove' the supernatural power of God that is so much needed in our present world of darkness. Until it is all for Jesus, all we are and have and ever hope to be, all of our ambitions, hopes and plans, until they are all surrendered, we will never walk in the real power of God. We are most often too attached to ourselves that we have remained detached from the supernatural. Until we are willing to come out of ourselves, we will continue to walk in illusion. Until like Paul, we are ready to count all things but loss, we will remain as natural as everybody and irrelevant to our generation.

One time, Paul became persuaded by the Spirit of God that his stepping into Jerusalem meant bonds and affliction for him. But instead of him deciding against Jerusalem, hear what this fearless apostle said:

"But none of these things move me, neither count I my life dear unto myself" Acts 20:24.

Even when genuine prophecy from the Lord came clearly warning the apostle of what awaited him at Jerusalem and the brethren were also weeping and trying to persuade Paul not to go to Jerusalem, hear his answer to them:

"I am ready not to be bound only, but also to die at Jerusalem for the name of the Lord Jesus" Acts 21:13.

Such is the kind of man that Paul was, and such are the kind of men God is still looking for today to be empowered to change our world for His glory. No wonder, that Paul had so much access into the realm of the supernatural in his life time and did what many of his contemporaries and those who were there before him could not do!

You can make up your mind as you go through this book to lay everything about your life on the altar and I assure you that your story can be told if another Bible were to be written.

CHAPTER THREE

THE PACKAGE OF ANOINTING

Several sincere Christians seeking to contact and walk in the supernatural do not really know how and where to reach it. Remember that the power we are talking about as we have noted earlier in chapter one can only be caught from on high (Luke 24:49) where God Himself Who is the Author of the supernatural dwells. We did also say that all power belongs to God (psalm 62:11), which means, one of God's attributes is power. It follows then, that God is an embodiment of power and whosoever wants to receive and demonstrate His power must first of all seek Him Who possesses the power.

The question that begs an answer then, is how do we seek God Who is a Spirit (John 4:24) and Who dwells in the supernatural, when we are natural men? Jesus says in John 6:63 that:

"The words that I have spoken to you, they are full of spirit and life" (NIV)

From the above scripture, we are told that the word of God is 'spirit' and 'life'. If the word of God is spirit and God Himself is a Spirit, it means that God and His word are both in the same realm (spirit realm). But in John 1:1, the bible says;

"In the beginning, was the Word, and the Word was with God, and the Word was God".

The above scripture shows us that the word of God is not only with God but is God Himself. Since the natural man cannot contact God Who is a Spirit (1Corrinthians 2:14), God now decides to make Himself available to us through His revealed word. So that anybody seeking to encounter Him can do that through His word which is a direct expression of God. The man who desires to operate in the supernatural therefore, must be one who has caught this revelation that one of the ways the power of God that we need to reveal the resurrected Christ to our dying world is through the living word of God.

THE WORD OF GOD IS THE CAPSULE OF GOD'S POWER

If you want to enjoy the fullness of God's power and bear God's glory in your generation, you must be an intense student of the word of God (the bible), because the word of God is the package of the anointing. You must continually soak up yourself in the word until you can't even see the pages any more. The inks on the pages are just letters and have no life in themselves, "for the letter kills, but the spirit gives life" (2Corrinthians 3:6). Until you are carried beyond the pages of the Bible, you cannot have an encounter with the supernatural. There is a river beyond the letter of the word unto which you can break as God takes the veil off your understanding. An incessant prayerful study of the word can introduce you into depths of God's unfathomable power and glory. Listen to what God says concerning His word in proverbs. 3:20:

"By His knowledge the depths are broken up, and the clouds drop down the dew".

Every obstacle to the power of God can be broken through revelation from His word. When a man comes out of the ocean of the word, he becomes an expression of God to his environment. Smith Wigglesworth said that; "The word of God changes a man until he becomes an epistle of God"

That statement is true for every genuine seeker of God through His word. Smith Wigglesworth was a living proof of Christ resurrection power in his time. It was said of him that after the apostle, Paul, there was no other person who demonstrated the power of the risen Christ like him. It however amazes me sometimes when I see men who say they are looking for the power of God but then they are so far and unfriendly with the word of God. Show me a man that has ever proved the power of God in his time, and I will show you a word-addicted-Christian.

John, the Baptist was a living proof of the supernatural, because he had an encounter with the word of God (Luke 3:2). Paul demonstrated that Christ is alive after he had encountered God's word on his way to Damascus (Acts 9:3-4), and all the prophets were men who were constantly in tune with the word of God.

The problem with so many of us is that we are often carried away with Christian literatures, that we have neglected the word of God to the detriment of our suffering world. A personal revelation from the Word is more powerful than what you could gather from all the books written by men put together. I am not in any way saying that reading books written by genuine servants of God is not important, because I am an addict of Christian books myself. But I am saying that reading other Christian literatures shouldn't be at the expense of our relationship with the word of God. This is extremely important. Other people's materials may give us some insight into the supernatural, but to a very limited extent.

PREMATURE ANOINTING IS A DISASTER

Friends, any anointing without a commensurate knowledge of the word of God is a premature anointing and the result can be disastrous. Somebody said that "premature responsibility breeds superficiality". All your zeal and quest for the supernatural without the knowledge of the word cannot take you far. It is actually important to be zealous. Every believer needs an initial zeal, because it is zeal that introduces us into seeking for more of God. But zeal must bring us to a point where the knowledge of God's word takes over. Many who started with great zeal for God never went far because they neglected the word.

Men like Samson in the Bible had zeal but untutored anointing. He perished on the way because of his lack of understanding of the anointing he was carrying. How do we get the understanding of the anointing but through the word of God? My father in the Lord, Pastor Ameh Amana once said that, "knowledge is the polisher of the anointing".

Williams Braham, a man described by many as "a man with notable signs and wonders" became a doctrinal disaster in his day and time because though he had a great healing and prophetic ministry, we are told he lacked the knowledge of the word of God to match it. Though he is in heaven by God's grace, his error is still very imminent among his followers. Lack of the knowledge of the word of God can make you a nuisance in the anointing. I pray that the Lord will help you.

CHAPTER FOUR

THE FULNESS OF TIME

One serious problem I have discovered with many of us believers is our inability to wait for God's fullness. We are too impatient and hasty that we cannot wait to receive what God has in store for us for our generation before we move. As soon as we start noticing a little mercy drops on our lives, we think we have got it and we haste away from his presence only to realize to our shame that we are empty. We ought to know that the supernatural does not come in a relay race.

The journey into the supernatural is a long distance journey. Only those who are patient run it. Such always go gently, but steadily and they go with a great attention. They keep mounting up momentum until they finally reach their destination in the supernatural. But those who want a short distance anointing start with speed, but after a while, they get tired and retired.

Several ministers of God today are already tired, about to drop their Bibles, because they never waited for the fullness of God's time before they moved out. And many also because they cannot wait for the authentic, they have decided to find an alternative to the power of God. In case you are of those who want to give up, I want to assure you that this book is meant to re- fire you in the name of Jesus.

THE LASTING POWER

In God's arrangement, there is what is called 'fullness of time'. God does not work outside of His fullness of time. God is never in haste in His programs. He never hurries and he is never flurried. He has a calendar which He faithfully follows. To send the Savior to the world, He waited for the fullness of time (Gal. 4:4). For John the Baptist, the forerunner of the Savior to be born, He made Elizabeth barren until the fullness of time. God always waits for the fullness of time. He makes all things beautiful in their season (Ecclesiastes. 3:11). Anything done outside the fullness of time is never beautiful and never lasts.

TEN DAYS FOR THE DISCIPLES.

Before the disciples got endued with the power that lasted them all their life time, they had to wait patiently for the fullness of God's time. With all their zeal to win the world for Jesus, they never moved until heaven had proved and approved them. We are told that they were in the upper room at Jerusalem (Acts 1:13) for about ten days before the power came. The truth is that if they had left the upper room on the ninth day, they would have still left without anything. But the Bible says "they continued with one accord in prayer and supplication" (Acts 1:14). So to catch the supernatural, we must learn to continue to wait until we have touched the power.

It's actually not an easy thing to wait. It requires a lot of discipline to wait. It is naturally very tedious to wait to get anything from God. But when we make up our minds, God makes the grace available. When you are sure of the promises of God, you are enabled to wait until you receive them. I am sure, the disciples must have had initial difficulty when they went into the upper room. Some of them must have even thought they were going to be there for only two or three days. But after waiting for two, three, four, five days and nothing happened, they knew they were in for a big business. God having proved their patience, the mark of their seriousness, heaven now responded on the tenth day.

"And when the day of Pentecost was fully come, they were all with one accord in one place. And suddenly there came a sound from heaven as of a rushing mighty wind, and it filled all the house where they were sitting" Acts 2:1-2.

Hear what the word of God says! They waited until "the day of Pentecost was fully come". That means God was waiting for a day to answer their prayers and it was "the day of Pentecost". And I want you to know also that there is a day that God is waiting for, to manifest you. I pray that you will not run ahead before that day comes and also that you will not miss the day when it finally comes in Jesus' name.

I want to draw your attention to the 'b' part of verse one. It says: "they were all with one accord in one place". They were not moving about. So many of us cannot sit for long in one place to hear what the Lord has for us. Everyone who desires to encounter the supernatural must learn the act of sitting in the presence of God. Many brethren are going about ministering with virtually nothing in them. A prophet can only declare what he has been told in God's secret place. It is what you receive in the secret place that makes you bold in the public. It was said concerning Jesus that any time He taught the word, "the people were astonished at His doctrine" (Matthew7:28). Why were the people always astonished at His teaching? Because, "He taught them as One having authority, and not as the scribes" (Matthew7:29). Now what is the difference between Jesus and the scribes. Very simple! Jesus taught from what He received in the spirit while He waited on God, but the scribes taught from the letters on their scroll.

What you do with God in the secret determines what you do for people in public. A man of God once said that, "your inward ministry unto God determines your outward ministry unto men"

Many of our pulpits are full of gimmicks because we have refused to wait upon God to brood over our lives. A man is not to be listened to, if he has not listened to God himself. A Christian who wants to experience what happened to the disciples in the book of Acts, i.e. "a mighty rushing wind" must be ready to wait for the fullness of time. Such experience is not easily come by.

MY LITTLE EXPERIENCE

I remember what happened to me in February, 1998 when my mother- fellowship then was waiting on the Lord in fasting for the whole of the month of February. Something happened to me that changed my mentality about the dealings of God. On the first five to six days of the fast, I was expecting an immediate supernatural visitation from God, but nothing happened significantly. In fact, after almost a week into the fasting program, nothing really showed up in my spirit as a proof that I was observing a fast. I was actually almost getting discouraged when suddenly, on the sixteenth day, heavens were opened unto me and I was inspired to write so many things that were beyond my spiritual age. In fact at a point, I became afraid of the hand of God that was heavy upon me. My little gift of writing today is actually a product of that encounter.

Now, if I had been discouraged and had stopped the fast, I would have no doubt missed that wonderful experience. This is just a little experience compared to what God desires to release upon His people in this last days if we really wait on Him. I'm telling you what just happened to me when I was still very young in the faith, and I know many have experienced such things before. I'm only trying to make us understand that waiting for the fullness of time requires great patience.

INSIST ON SHOWERS

Whenever you are burdened to wait on God for a particular visitation for a particular period of time, always insist on the best from the Lord. When you notice some drops of mercy, quickly thank God for that, but never be satisfied with mercy drops, for it will not be enough for you and your generation. There is a shower of God's rain that awaits you if you continue to insist on the best. My own prayer everyday has been "others may be satisfied with mercy drops, but not me. I must wait for the showers". I don't want to be half-baked. Have-baked Christians will always turn back in the day of battle (Psalm 78:9), and I don't want to turn back from the battle front, because I was called to be a fighter and not a quitter, knowing that it is only a fighter who always wins and not a quitter.

WE HAVE DIFFERENT CALENDERS WITH GOD

Don't you ever compare yourself with any other person. You may begin the journey of faith the same day with somebody. You must know that your days of manifestation may be different. Our spiritual calendar is different from one another. God knows the best time to introduce us to our generation. It was said of John, the Baptist that he was in the deserts until the day of his showing forth (Luke 1:80). What I mean here is that, in as much as we desire the supernatural, we will also do well to be sensitive to God's timing, because when it is God's season, it becomes easy. It saves us a whole lot of stress. I repeat what I have said earlier on, that is, the supernatural is a long distance journey. Some may get there before the others, but everybody can get there if we exercise a little patience. Somebody said that, "even the snail the slowest of animals made it to the Ark that Noah built". I believe the snail also made it to the ark because of its persistence and perseverance. So, if the snail could make it to the Ark despite its slowness, even you can make it to the supernatural if you are patient. It's a matter of time!

CATCHING THE SUPERNATURAL

When Elisha started his journey of the supernatural, many never believed he would amount to anything. All he was doing for years was just pouring water on the hand of Elijah, his master and running errand for him (2Kings. 3:11). But quietly and patiently, he was gathering experience and momentum for his time of manifestation as his master took him from one stage of experience to another. Those who called themselves sons of prophets studying theology and analyzing prophecies were ridiculing him. But he was not deterred, because he was too conscious of the supernatural to be distracted.

THE RESULT OF WAITING

When Elisha and his master Elijah went over the Jordan where God was going to snatch Elijah away, he now gave opportunity to Elisha to ask whatever he wanted him to do for him. Listen to me, when you wait for the fullness of time, God will definitely speak. When we wait, all the resources of heaven will be at our disposal. Ours is just to ask and we will receive. Elisha had waited patiently for these years and it is now his turn to ask for the power. Let's see how Elisha asked for the supernatural:

"When they had crossed, Elijah said to Elisha, Tell me what Can I do for you before I am taken from you?" "Let me inherit A double portion of your spirit," Elisha replied 2 Kings 2:9.

Elisha's answer shows that he had been out for a great deal. He really meant the supernatural. He was not even afraid to carry the double portion of what Elijah his master had walked in. Because he knew that Elijah's anointing will be too insufficient for his own generation. He knew that Elijah's anointing was no longer sufficient to deal with that godless woman, Jezebel who had held Israel in spiritual hostage for many years, so he needed a double portion to deal with her and her powers. This is important for us to know. The reason why it is necessary for us to wait for the fullness of God is because the rate of the devil's operation in our generation is greater compared to what it used to be. We need all the anointing of men of old put together to be able to capture our present wicked world for our God.

There are too many manifestations of the devil around today that we cannot afford to operate in the periphery of power. We need the center of the supernatural. Let's now see the response of the soon-to-be taken man of God to his servant, Elisha's demand of double portion:

"You have asked a difficult thing, Elijah said", 2 kings 2:10a.

HARD BUT POSSIBLE

I told us before that the supernatural is always hard to attain. It is not a thing for babies. It is not for the lily liver, nor for the faint-hearted. Yes, it is difficult, but it is possible to catch, yet only if you pay the price. Here's the condition for it: "Yet if you see me when I am taken from you, it will be yours- otherwise, it will not" 2 Kings 2:10b (NIV)

The condition given to Elisha for him to receive the supernatural was "if you see me when I am taken from you." This is talking about being constantly conscious of the supernatural. If we must operate in this realm, we must be people who can 'see' beyond the natural, because what you can't see, you can't receive, and what you can't picture, you can't capture. In the journey into the supernatural, there are many distractions on the way. Many things will be craving for your attention. The aim is to get you miss the supernatural, so that will live an empty and ordinary life. Elisha clearly got the message and he made up his mind not to miss this glorious encounter. I pray, you will not miss it.

"As they were walking along and talking together, suddenly a chariot of fire and horses of fire appeared and separated the two of them, and Elijah went up to heaven in a whirlwind" 2Kings 2:11(NIV)

As Elisha was waiting, suddenly, the supernatural began to happen. Elijah who was once in the natural is being translated into the supernatural before his eyes. So Elisha made up his mind that though he was not going to go with Elijah into the supernatural, he must partake in the supernatural. And the only way to succeed in that was to steadfastly look on Elijah who was being translated before his eyes. And so Elisha who was in the natural began to behold what was happening in the supernatural. I want to say that heavens can be opened unto us if we insist on the supernatural. Many times, we are too satisfied with the natural, which is why the supernatural has eluded us for years, so God must wake us to the consciousness of the supernatural again, because our world is dying, because we have nothing in our hands to save them.

Because, Elisha has been forewarned, though the sight was fearful, he refused to remove his eyes from heaven. And as he continued to behold, the supernatural was released to him via the mantle of Elijah and "He took up also the mantle of Elijah that fell from him, and went back" 2Kings. 2:13 (NIV)

Please, don't go back to the field, until you have caught the supernatural! Don't go back to the battle without the mantle. Don't go and face the world with an empty hand. Nations are waiting for you to be manifested, don't disappoint them. By the time Elisha had caught the mantle and returned, all those who had ridiculed him began to welcome him saying:

"The company of the prophets from Jericho, who were watching, said, 'The spirit of Elijah is resting on Elisha. "And they went to meet him, and bowed to the ground before him" 2kings 2:15 (NIV).

If we wait for the fullness of time, those who ignore us will begin to recognize us. When God shall have responded to our patience, we shall be celebrated by those who once rejected us. Though Elisha never went to Bible school, when he returned from the pursuit of the supernatural, those in the school of prophecy all became his students (Read 2kings 6). After reading this book, your life will never remain the same. You will become a wonder to your generation in Jesus' name.

CHAPTER FIVE

WHEN THE POWER COMES

How do you know when the power comes and how do you know when you have contacted the power? Well, in the case of the disciples, when it came, there was a rushing mighty wind. You might not experience a physical rushing wind in your case, but it is going to be evident that from the moment you contact the power, your life will be full of a rushing mighty experiences. Let's now take a look at the various experiences that began to accompany the disciples when the power came in the upper room. Acts 2:1-8 state that:

1. "When the day of Pentecost came, they were all together in one place. 2. Suddenly a sound like the blowing of a violent wind came from heaven and filled the whole house where they were sitting. 3. They saw what seemed to be tongues of fire that separated and came to rest on each of them. 4. All of them were filled with the Holy Spirit and began to speak in other tongues as the Spirit enabled them.5. Now there were staying in Jerusalem God-fearing Jews from every nation under heaven. 6. When they heard this sound, a crowd came together in bewilderment, because each one heard their own language being spoken. 7. Utterly amazed, they asked: 'Aren't all these who are speaking Galileans? Then how is it that each of us hears them in our native language?" (NIV)

THE EVIDENCE OF POWER

From the above text we saw about six different experiences that began to accompany them, namely:

1. **Abundant Revelations:** from vs. 3, we saw that as soon as the wind of Pentecost began to blow on the disciples, "They saw what seemed to be tongues of fire". This depicts divine revelation. The disciples began to see what they have never seen before. They were

granted access to see beyond the natural. They began to behold the extra-ordinary. Remember, these were ordinary men like you and I. Some of them were mere fishermen who were not recognized by the religious gurus of their time. They were ordinary unschooled Jewish citizens. But the wind of glory began to translate them into the supernatural to see "the deep things of God" (1Corrinthians 2:10).

This is the kind of experience that will accompany anyone who avails himself to God for the supernatural. This is the kind of revelation we need to enable us interpret the supernatural to the natural men around us. Our world like the world of Daniel is in dire need of interpreters of their dreams, and only the supernaturally empowered can do that. Our world is waiting for Josephs to interpret the dreams of their Pharaohs. Only those in touch with the supernatural can dissolve the doubts of men. The bible says, unto us the followers of Christ are given to know the mysteries of the kingdom of God. Men and women will continue to live in miseries, until their mysteries are unraveled by us. We cannot afford to disappoint heaven and our world because we have been given the key to set the world free from the bondage of corruption (Romans 8:21).

Several errors abound in the Body of Christ today because of the lack of divine revelation. Where there is no revelation, men take a little thing they know and build a doctrine out of it. When there is divine revelation, we no longer do ministry with struggle because we do only what we see our Father in heaven do (John 5:19).

Paul the great apostle succeeded in the ministry because all the steps he took during his ministry were by revelation. For example, at the beginning of his letter to the Galatians, he made them to understand that his call was not by man but by God: "Paul, an apostle, not of men, neither by man, but by Jesus Christ" (Gal. 1:1 KJV).

In another place, Paul stated that he took a journey to Jerusalem and this journey was not in assumption, but according to him, "I went up by revelation" (Galatians 2:2 KJV). Revelation makes the work of God easier to do.

2. **A Personal Fire:** Acts 2:3 reveals that the revelation of the fire which they had was not just corporate. The fire that was released from heaven came on them individually. When the power comes, there must be a personal experience of the fire. The bible says, the fire sat upon each of them. Christians in our days are often satisfied with congregational experience. Such people come back from meetings with stories of the move of God without God moving their lives an inch. This is very sad, because, it is what you have experienced as an individual that you will be able to offer your generation. Your relevance is in your personal encounters with the supernatural and not in corporate encounters. Don't misunderstand me. Corporate encounters are equally important. They will challenge you to

seek more of God, But am saying that only that which you experience with God personally is the key for personal relevance.

3. **A resident Fire:** Acts 2:3 also reveal that the revelation of the fire which they had was not just a momentary experience,   that is to say that the fire that came did not come to depart. It came to stay. The Bible says, "it sat upon... them". The fire that came did not come as a visitor, but as a resident (read also John 1:33). That means every one of them in the upper room left there a carrier of God's holy fire. We should not be satisfied with any experience less than an experience that comes to be part of us. Though some times as we labor in the field the fire reduces in intensity, but when we have it resident in us, it can be renewed from God's presence for a greater exploit. Because, even the disciples after receiving this experience, they still came to God's presence from time to time for a renewal, when they noticed a decrease in their effectiveness (Acts 4:23-31).

The point I'm trying to stress is that never should we be content with the fire that visits only when we are in a congregation and depart thereafter. That is but an emotional experience. That cannot take us anywhere. May God give you a permanent and a resident fire for a lasting ministry in the name Jesus.

4. **Speaking in other tongues:** I decided to include this for the sake of Christians who are still struggling with the issue of baptism in the Holy Ghost and speaking in other tongues either because they are ignorant of this phenomenon or they have been deceived by their denomination that this experience is not for our days. In case you belong to any of these categories, never mind because it is not your fault. By the time you are through with this book, you will not only receive enough revelation to believe that it is for you, but you shall also be filled in Jesus' name. So let's go together to Acts 2:4. It says,

"All of them were filled with the Holy Spirit and began to speak in other tongues as the Spirit enabled them" (NIV).

Please note that as soon as the wind of Pentecost began to blow in the room where they were sitting, the Bible says that "all of them were filled with the Holy Spirit". I know many people don't have problem with this part, that is the filling with the Holy Ghost and I know you too reading this book may not have much problem here. This is because many argue that all Christians are filled with Holy Ghost as at the time of salvation. I agree with such people to a certain limit. Because, you remember that the disciples in question here long before now were all already born again followers of Christ. That means they have been filled with Holy Ghost even before now.

The question now is this, why should the disciples need any further filling of the Holy Ghost? The question will answer itself as we press on. You will agree with me that if the disciples who had been with Jesus these years and had seen His power still needed another filling, it means there is something significant to this second filling that we need to find out. Let's look at Acts 2:4 together again:

"All of them were filled with the Holy Spirit and began to speak in other tongues as the Spirit enabled them"

Do you see that the story does not just end with the filling with the Holy Ghost but that this new filling added another dimension to their lives that is the speaking with other tongues? This is the experience that gave them the needed power for effective ministry and walk with God. And except you desire to remain a mediocre you need this power. But if you really want to make your mark as far as the kingdom of God is concerned, then you need this experience as quickly as possible. All you need to do is just cry unto God with a sincere heart and deal with every known sin and He will fill you.

I also do not want to leave you in the dark concerning the fact that there are a lot of abuses or misuse of this great experience in the church today. This is because many Christians want to be identified with the supernatural without laboring for it. There are several manipulations by Christians of this experience. Some even practice now how to speak in tongues and they come to display it in the public and some are taught by others. These are mere manipulation of the power of God. But, the fact that there are counterfeit should not make us discard the real.

One truth remains; that counterfeit can only exist where the real thing exists. You can't talk of counterfeit money, if there is no genuine money. In fact, it is because Christianity is so real and heavenly that Satan is counterfeiting it in several ways possible. So friend, this experience of speaking in other tongues is no less real and heavenly than your salvation experience. All we need to do is to learn to be acquainted with the original. Because, if you are used to the original, you can't be deceived by an imitation.

5. **Holy Spirit guided message:** Remember, we are still looking at some of the experiences that attended the ministries of the disciples when the power came. Looking at Acts 2:4 again, the Bible says:

"All of them were filled with the Holy Spirit and began to speak in other tongues as the Spirit enabled them".

You discover that as soon as the power came on them, all their words were being guided. The bible says, they spoke "as the Spirit enabled them". The King James Version says, "as the Spirit gave them utterance". This is an experience we all need to be able to speak the mind of God. The prophets of old never spoke unless as they were mandated and enabled

(Ezekiel. 37:7, 10). Such Spirit led message is accompanied with accuracy because you never speak except as you are permitted to speak.

One of the things that enhanced the earthly ministry of our Lord Jesus Christ was His ability to hear from God at all times. He never spoke until He had heard God. He never judged until He had heard God. He was always in harmony with the Spirit of Truth (Jn. 5:30).

One thing that has brought about so much doubtful ministries today in the Body of Christ is inability of God's people to really discern the mind of God for their time. We go around speaking from our own spirits. We gave words of prophecy that are not Bible-based. Many of us are like the false prophets of Jeremiah's days who said "Thus saith the Lord" when God has not said anything (Jeremiah. 23:1-40). I wish we go back to God with sincere hearts to receive from Him before we come out to declare His word. Paul boasted to the Corinthian church that his visit to them was not with "wise and persuasive words but with a demonstration of the Spirit's power" 1Cor. 2:1, 4 (NIV).

As soon as the power comes, you will know because your tongue will change. Your language will change from the one it used to be. Your language will change from the language of the flesh to that of the Spirit. It will no longer be you in charge of your tongue but the Holy Ghost. The Holy Ghost takes over and you now speak as He directs. Everybody will know that you have contacted the supernatural by your new utterance. You no longer struggle with words when you stand to preach the word of God. Even your prayer is now controlled by the Holy Ghost. The words freely come as you dare to open your mouth. This has nothing to do with either your education or what you have practiced. This is purely the work of the Spirit of God in action.

Your experience will become as the Psalmist puts it "open wide your mouth and I will fill it" (Psalm 81:10). Oh, what wonderful prophets of God we will all become, if we truly contact this experience. The Spirit of the Lord is coming again upon His church. Let's all position ourselves at the right place for Him to locate us.

5. **God's introduction:** Another thing that happened to the ministries of the disciples when the fire came was that they were introduced by God and the noise of their ministries went abroad: "Now when this was noised abroad, the multitude came together" Acts 2:6(NIV)

The fame of their ministry went beyond the shore of Jerusalem as soon as they contacted the supernatural. They never printed any invitation. They never even arranged for any public address systems, but God gave them approval by introducing them. The bible says concerning Jesus that the reason why He did all He did in His ministries was that He was "a

Man approved of God among you" (Acts 2:22). It was not because of publicity or His connection. It was that He was approved of God.

When I see people placing so much emphasis on equipments, it amazes me because it looks now to us as if God cannot do His works if these things are not available. As much as equipments are important to us today, their absence cannot hinder the work of God. Listen, if you are not approved by God, the result of all your efforts in trying to show yourself would just be equal to hay and wood that would soon be consumed. I tell you the truth, if God's power is present, the absence of many things cannot be noticed.

What happened when their noise went abroad? The Bible says: "the multitude came together" (vs. 6). Who brought the multitude? It was God and not handbills. When God gives a man a genuine ministry, He always prepares a multitude that will listen to him from anywhere whether invited or not. Many preachers are making connections on how to travel abroad by all means when the noise of their ministry has not even reached the members of their own immediate family. Some zealous brethren argue that in this age, it is not possible for preachers to travel abroad unless they have possessed some certificates from a recognized bible school. I totally disagree with that kind of reasoning, because if God actually wants me to take the gospel to any nation of the world, He will make all the necessary connections that need to be made. In fact, if the noise of my ministry reaches abroad, the people who want me there will arrange for all the documents that will aid my journey to their country, it's as simple as that!

John the Baptist was in the wilderness and Pharisees, army generals and politicians all came to him begging him to address them on their salvation (Matt. 3:5, Lk. 3:7). Listen to me friends, multitude will gather to you when you wait on God for the great experience of Pentecost. Concerning John the Baptist, the Bible says:

"...the child grew, and waxed strong in spirit, and was in the deserts till the day of his shewing unto Israel" Luke 1:80 (NIV).

Hear me! There is a day in God's calendar called the day of your "showing forth". If you go before that day, you have no message from Him and you will soon become irrelevant. What happened when the multitude came together?

"Now when this was noised abroad, the multitude came together and were confounded" Acts 2:6(NIV)

The bible says the multitude that gathered around them was confounded. Why were they confounded? Because, they never expected such thing from these ordinary Jewish citizens. Among the multitude that came were the Pharisees and doctors of law who thought they knew everything about God. On seeing the disciples, they were confounded because they were seeing things beyond their intellectual capability. They were seeing the supernatural happening through these unlearned fishermen. Friends, if we allow God to work on our lives before we go forth, even the greatest of minds shall be confounded by our ministries.

6. **Chapter of miracles:** Finally, God opened another chapter for their lives and ministries after their encounter at the upper room. This time, it is the chapter of miracles. Remember, I said earlier on in chapter two that God is looking for men who can through the supernatural accomplish the impossible. I want to add here that after this upper room experience, you will not only affect the spirits and souls of men, you will also begin to affect their physical conditions. Your life will become a testimony of miracles. There will be attestations of miraculous happenings here and there in your ministry and another chapter will be opened altogether for your life and ministry.

Note that after all that happened to the disciples in Acts 2, God opened another chapter for Peter and John in Acts 3. This time, it was the chapter of physical miracles, testifying to the word which they had declared in chapter two. Beloved, the chapter two of your ministry is only the chapter of the word. There's another chapter after the word and that is the chapter of spectacular and miraculous manifestations. The gospel of the Lord Jesus is a wholesome gospel. It is for the total man (spirit, soul and body). Your ministry is not complete if the physical conditions of men are not addressed. As one preacher puts it: "The miraculous is surely a dimension that cannot be divorced from the gospel".

PHILIP IN SAMARIA

"Then Philip went down to Samaria, and preached Christ unto them. And the people with one accord gave heed unto those things which Philip spake, hearing and seeing the miracles which he did" Acts 8:5-6.

When Philip went to Samaria in an evangelistic campaign, his message was directed to the total man, as a result, miraculous happenings attested his ministry and we are told that:

"the people with one accord gave heed unto those things which Philip spake" Acts 8:6a

What was it that stirred up their faith? Was it only what Philip spoke that made them believe? Was it only the great exposition of the scriptures that brought them to repentance? Of course, not. For the same Acts 8:6b says: "hearing and seeing the miracles which he did". Verse 7 enumerates some of the manifestations that created faith on the inside of these people. "For unclean spirits, crying with loud, voice came out of many that were possessed with them: and many taken with palsies, and that were lame, were healed"

No wonder, the Bible says: "And there was great joy in that city" (vs. 8). What city is the bible talking about? The city that saw the God that cared even for their physical conditions.

Our generation wants to see God confirm His word with miraculous signs. I am not saying that it is only through miracles that God can bring men to repentance. After all, God is a sovereign God. He can do all things. But I am saying that the God that we serve cares for our every need. Even the Master himself testified in John 4:48 that some may not believe unless they see signs and wonders. I am aware that many of us are actually struggling with the miraculous. But the fact that many ministries are not experiencing it does not negate the fact that we need it. I am convinced that as we wait patiently on God, every one of us will experience the supernatural, because it is our heritage in Christ Jesus.

BUT THIS SIGNS SHALL FOLLOW

How did the disciples come about the miraculous dimension of their ministries in chapter three and other chapters of the book of Acts? The bible says:

"And they went forth, and preached everywhere, the Lord working with them, and confirming the word with signs following them" Mark 16:20.

They did not just sit down after the experience of Pentecost. "They went forth". The Pentecost experience is not for sitting, it is for moving. So if a new chapter must be opened for you, then you must be on the move with the gospel and expect signs to confirm your message. This is the only way your ministry can be vindicated. You can't sit down and expect anything to happen. You must always be on the going. After all the spelling of our commission is 'go ye' (Matt. 28:19) and not 'sit ye'. Remember, that Jesus;

"went about doing good, and healing all that were oppressed of the devil, for God was with Him"Acts 10:38.

It was as He went about that He saw the needs of the people that spurred compassion in Him which brought healing to them. But don't forget this: He was able to succeed because God was with Him. Can I ask you? Is God with you? If not, then don't go until you have Him with you because it could be very dangerous and a colossal disaster if He is absent in your ministry.

Remember also that in Mark 16:17, Jesus promised that "these signs shall follow them that believe". The signs that Jesus promised is not a stagnant sign, it is a sign that moves. It is a sign that follows. It is a sign that accompanies. That means it follows only those that are on the move.

For example, in John 5, the Bible records that there was a great feast of the Jews going on in Jerusalem and everyone was going to enjoy themselves at the feast. It was natural for Jesus to be part of that feast. But when he came to Jerusalem, instead of going for the feast, He made His way to the pool of Bethesda where the needs abound. That was the custom of Jesus; He was always looking for people in trouble to give them a helping hand.

Many of us are too occupied with temple activities that our ministries have terminated in our chapter two. While thousands are out there bound in chains of darkness waiting for the glorious manifestation of the sons of God, unfortunately, the sons of God are busy celebrating feast in the temple. The sons of God are supposed to be moving temples. Scriptures say we are the temple of God (1Corrinthians 3:16 and 6:19). Many of us never know that God has changed His habitation more than two thousand years ago. He used to be in the temple in Jerusalem, but when the Holy Ghost came at Pentecost, God relocated into the life of every believer in Christ and so you and I are now the temples of God and we are not stationary or dead temples like the temple in Jerusalem. We are moving and living temples. I trust God that after going through the pages of this book, you will no longer be satisfied with ordinary church activities. Rather you will begin to seek the face of God for the supernatural that will usher you into the chapter three of your life and ministry.

In all our hunger and thirst after the reality of the power of God in our lives and ministries, we must not forget that the only inevitable factor that will guarantee our sustenance in the power of God is the mercy of God. We must not come to any place in our walk with God that we begin to take His mercy for granted. Outside the mercy of God we are just mere men. The greatest of men are great only because of His mercy and the wisest of men are only wise because of His mercy. If you dare downplay the mercy of God, He quietly withdraws Himself and the consequence of that can be terrible.

CHAPTER SIX

THE MERCY OF GOD

I am compelled to include this chapter because many of God's servants in time past who were greatly used of God were suddenly abandoned by God because they lost touch with the mercy of God at one point in their ministries. They came to a place where they thought they were succeeding by their own strength, only to realize that they were but limited mortal men when God withdrew.

TRUSTING IN HIS STRENGTH DAILY

No matter how long we have walked with God and how great we have become as a result of our wealth of experience, we must not allow it to get into our heads. What I mean is that we must not become too experienced to depend on God for our daily sustenance. Hear this: what we need for today's ministry cannot be found in yesterday's experience, for His mercies are new every morning (Lam. 3:23).

Remember, that in the wilderness, God allowed the children of Israel to gather manna only as much as they needed for every day (Ex. 16:16). There were those who tried God by gathering for two days, only to discover to their dismay that the ones gathered for the next day became worms (Ex. 16:20). I dare to caution that if your ministry must not become worms, you must look unto Him for daily renewal. And even in the Gospels, Jesus teaches us to pray only for our daily bread, nor our weekly or monthly or yearly bread (Matt. 6:11). This is so we can always lift up our eyes to Him on daily basis.

David, in all his experience and greatness learnt to depend on God for his daily sustenance. In the book of second Samuel chapter five, immediately David was made king over Israel, the Philistines gathered themselves to fight against him. One would have naturally expected King David who was so experienced in war to have gone ahead to fight the Philistines using his past and great experience of battle. But instead David went to God to inquire of Him on how to go about this battle;

"But when the Philistines heard that they had anointed David king over Israel, all the Philistines came up to seek David;.....And David enquired of the LORD, saying, shall I go up to the Philistines? Wilt thou deliver them into mine hand? And the LORD said unto David, Go up: for I will doubtless deliver the Philistines into thine hand" Vs.17 & 19

Having being assured by God of victory, he went and actually came back with victory at the word of God. How did he overcome? He obtained mercy from the Lord for the battle.

Having been defeated, the Philistines went and fortified themselves and came back again to fight David. David again knew that for another victory to be secured, he needed another mercy from the Lord. He knew that the Philistines he defeated in the first battle were quite different from these ones, hence the need for a new strategy for this entirely new battle. I tell you, this is the winning secret in life and ministry. When David went back to God to inquire of Him, He gave him another strategy entirely different from the one he used in the first battle (2 Sam. 5:23-23). Had David gone ahead to use the first strategy to fight the second battle, he would have faced a colossal defeat. The bible recorded that David never lost a single battle in all his life because he always depended on the mercy of God. How could he have defeated a giant like Goliath if not that he secured the mercy of God?

I am sure; it was this attitude of David that endeared him to God's heart which eventually earned him the title: "a man after God's heart"(Acts 13:22). I know God is no respecter of persons. If He sees men who will seek after Him today, He will still have today many men after His heart. Therefore, as God enlarges our scope of ministries by the day, we must also endeavor to seek Him for commensurate enlargement in His mercy.

THE SACRIFICES THE LORD REQUIRES

Sometimes, our confidence on our personal sacrifices can become a great obstacle in manifesting the supernatural power of God. Prayer and fasting are two great keys for unlocking the supernatural. They are very important exercises as far as the supernatural is concerned. Even Jesus told us that there are certain matters that cannot be handled in the ministry except by prayer and fasting (Matthew 17:21). And Jesus Himself engaged in a forty-day fast before He embarked on His earthly ministry.

But, I want to caution that sometimes, these exercises (prayer and fasting) as good as they are can become so idolized in our hearts that we may lose sight of God's mercy. We must remember that all our sacrifices outside the platform of His God's mercy are mere rituals. The real sacrifice that God is looking for is a broken spirit. "The sacrifices of God are a broken spirit" Psalm 51:17b.

God is not as much interested in our sacrifices as He is interested in our hearts. If we become proud in our ability, we scare God away. Anytime we begin to count on our efforts, we lose His supports, because God is not interested in able men. God is looking for men who are not able to enable them with His mercy. God always resist the proud in heart and gives grace to those who are humble. No amount of fasting and prayer can equal the grace of God. It's not by power nor by might but by the Spirit of the Lord (Zech. 4:6)

If God is actually too interested in our sacrifices, then so many of us would have been less than nothing in the kingdom, but as apostle Paul said: "But by the grace of God I am what I am" (1Corrithians 15:10). I have discovered that when I fast and pray, this is to enable me plunge into more of His mercy, and at the end of my prayer and fasting, I must not become confident in my prayer and fasting themselves, but in the fact that I have obtained mercy from the Lord during the exercise. Even the greatest of preachers can become nothing in the ministry when they begin to put their confidence in their own abilities.

May the hand of God descend and remain upon you even as you read through this book and may His grace be sufficient for you to remain a seeker of His presence always and may you obtain His mercy for every phase of your life and ministry in Jesus' name.

God bless you!